A Main Street Lawyer in the Early 1900s

A Main Street Lawyer in the Early 1900s

Harry H. Emmons

VANTAGE PRESS
New York

My Early 1900s Law Office on Main Street

To his beloved wife and helpmate,

Pauline Temple Emmons (1888–1981)

Foreword

Harry H. Emmons (1878–1952) wrote these memoirs in 1950. This autobiographical manuscript is dedicated to his beloved wife and helpmate, Pauline Temple Emmons (1888–1981), mother of their daughter (b. 1909) and son (b. 1919). His book is published here in loving memory. Editing has been kept to a minimum, but names have been changed.

—Richard Harrison Emmons (son)

A Main Street Lawyer
in the Early 1900s

Chapter I
A Case of Attempted Blackmail

Perhaps my story may give enlightenment and courage to some other lawyer, sometime, somewhere, who finds his efforts thwarted by similar powerful interests or a political dictator. I hope so.

Shortly after I was admitted to the bar in 1906, I established my law office on Main Street in a small midwestern city. I did not have much business the first few months, nor did I expect to have. It was the so-called "starving period" of the profession.

There were no rich relatives to give or send me business, but I did have enough patronage to keep me going. I was learning something every day—about the town and about business in general. I was getting a glimpse into practical politics, as well as acquainting myself with court procedures. One of the important things I learned was that our city had a political boss, a man who had inherited wealth, as well as the city's main newspaper. Every officer, from the mayor and city solicitor down, and every prospective candidate for local election was subservient to this political dictator, who managed and edited the newspaper he had inherited. He will be referred to hereafter as simply "the Boss."

The main reporter on this newspaper's staff had little regard for ethical journalism and had a habit of writing sensational stories, regardless of the facts. The reporter was quite irresponsible, owning no property, paying no taxes, and associating with questionable characters from whom he often got unreliable information for his stories. The Boss paid him twelve dollars per week. He was a friend of the Boss, and he often served as a front behind which the Boss could conceal his own personal responsibility. I did not know much about this reporter when I first opened my law office, but some months thereafter I happened to meet him on the street. We stopped and talked for a while. Then, to my surprise, he asked me for a loan of a few dollars for a week or two. As he was practically a stranger to me and I could not afford it, I should not have let him have the money. Yet I did grant his request. That was the beginning of trouble, as I tried repeatedly, without success, to get him to repay the money I had advanced to him. On the last occasion he showed his true character by threatening that if I should ever try to collect my claim, he would smear me in his columns at the first opportunity. That, of course, amounted to blackmail. I told him so in very caustic words, which made no impression on him. I did not know or even suspect then that he was skinning other local businessmen in the same manner, but I found out this was true. One of his victims was a Mr. S., from whom I later learned he had extracted $100. Notwithstanding the reporter's reputation among businessmen, he could get printed almost anything he desired, using his privilege for purely selfish purposes. Businessmen did not dare risk being made the victim of his poisoned pen. Therefore, more often than not they permitted themselves to be blackmailed. Apparently the Boss knew nothing about these private schemes. With this sort of a setup, no person could feel safe from the designs of this reporter.

Two years after I began my law practice, this reporter wrote a false and damaging story about a young married couple, bringing them into public scandal and disgrace. Someone recommended that they should see me. After they told me their story and explained, with tears in their eyes, how this false story would affect their standing in the community, I believed they had a meritorious claim for damages. They needed the services of an attorney. I partly realized what it might mean to me to accept their cases, but I agreed to represent them in court. Accordingly, I filed suit in the Common Pleas Court for damages. I was fully aware that this newspaper corporation, through its Boss, would do almost anything to win these cases. My clients were young and unsophisticated, so I did warn them that during the pendency of these suits they must "watch their step" and look out for pretended new friends who might really be snooping detectives. My clients seemed to understand what I was talking about, and they promised to keep my warning and advice in mind. Afterward I found out that they evidently did not fully comprehend what I was trying to tell them.

One day a fine-looking young woman, perhaps twenty-five years of age, came into my office and introduced herself as Miss Helen Harter of Detroit. She said she was thinking of locating in our city and opening a beauty salon; that she was consulting various business and professional men and had come to seek my advice in the matter. I told her that I knew nothing about such matters and could give her no worthwhile opinion. But she generously offered to pay me for the time I gave her. Of course, I did not accept anything. She thanked me profusely and left. It was a mere incident that I soon forgot, but a few days later she called again, explaining that a check she was expecting had not arrived and asking me to advance her a few dollars for a few days. She offered to leave with me, as security, her diamond ring. I believed her story and loaned her the money. After she left, however, it occurred to me that this request coupled with the first call was queer and singular. The more I thought about it, the more I became convinced that something was wrong. It did not add up. Then I thought of a straightforward, honest private detective—someone very valuable to know at times. I sent for him and put him on Miss Harter's track.

My detective was quite efficient, smooth, and effectual. He kept me informed on everything that was going on. In due time Miss Harter came in, repaid the money I had advanced, and thanked me again most profusely for this little favor. It seemed to me that she wanted to be too friendly, and she unnecessarily played up her pulchritudinous charms. From then on she called at my office every few days, but before the next time she came in I knew all about her. I played innocent, but I was angry enough to strike her. I could hardly restrain this impulse at various times thereafter, yet I realized that I dare not do anything radical that would play directly into the hands of the conspirators about whom I will soon explain.

Starting at this time I confided fully in my wife and a few close friends about the nefarious affair then in the making. Of course I was shocked, and the others in whom I confided were also shocked. It amounted to an attempt to ruin my home, seriously affecting my wife and our small daughter. Thinking it over carefully, I decided to continue playing gullible. I would bide my time for the purpose of later exposing the scheme and, if possible, sending the guilty parties to the penitentiary.

My detective, under the guise of being a vicious enemy of mine, carefully wormed himself into the good graces and full confidence of the two men detectives aiding this female, John Adams and Ed Gilson. My detective faithfully reported to me almost every day. He discovered and explained in detail that there was a deliberately planned scheme to blackmail me into dropping lawsuits pending against this newspaper, whose owner, the Boss, was directing the proceedings and furnishing all the money needed. He had in collaboration the two men, John Adams and Ed Gilson, as well as at least one of the attorneys representing the newspaper in the libel suits I had initiated. The Boss even had Adams and Gilson pretend to establish a detective agency. They opened an office nearby on Main Street with "Detective Agency" painted on the front windows and office door, and an article in the newspaper announcing the opening of this agency was printed. The office purported to be a legitimate concern for general detective work, whereas in truth and fact it was only a make-believe organization for the sole purpose of snaring me and my clients! This elaborate setup was a precaution the Boss was taking to have an alibi ready if necessary or expedient to claim that he had simply hired legitimate detectives and was himself innocent of any wrongdoing. In short, the Boss wanted to get rid of this one and only pesky lawyer who had the nerve to challenge his impregnability and prestige by filing suits against his newspaper.

My detective worked into the scheme without arousing their suspicion, but had his part been discovered by the Boss's henchmen I feel sure he would have been in a very dangerous position. I never publicly revealed his identity, although I needed his testimony in the litigation that followed. Just how I had found out so many things I revealed in court was beyond the comprehension of the conspirators, as they had thought their secret operations were airtight.

I was aware that a lawyer sometimes should not trust his own client with information, plans, or suspicions for his client's own good, as illustrated by the following incident. One day Mrs. Mills, my client in one of these libel suits against the Boss's newspaper, came into my office to ask what was developing in regard to her case. After a little conversation I asked her if she was observing my caution about being careful. She assured me that she was.

Then I said, "I happened to see you on the street the other day with a strange woman. Who was she?"

"Oh," she said, "that was Miss Harter, who

stays over at our rooming house. Why do you ask?"

All I could say was, "Oh, I just wondered." I had not really seen her with this woman, but my detective had, and I had asked the question to get her reaction. "Well," I continued, "remember I told you to be careful," and then I changed the subject. At the time I did not dare to entrust her with the knowledge that I knew Miss Harter was a dangerous blackmailing detective.

About two days later, the so-called Miss Harter visited me again. After talking a few minutes about trivial matters, she suddenly asked, "What is this, Mr. Emmons, about you telling Mrs. Mills that I am a detective?"

I had to think fast and pretend to be not at all disturbed by this disturbing question, and said, "Oh, you surely are mistaken, because I never said anything of that kind to Mrs. Mills. I often do tell clients, in important cases, that they should be careful of their conduct and not to mix too freely with strangers, and Mrs. Mills perhaps misunderstood me. But I surely never told her that you were a detective."

This evidently disarmed her, and if she later did ask Mrs. Mills about it, as she probably did, Mrs. Mills could and would have verified my statement. All her suspicions must have been allayed, as shown by her continued machinations.

A few days thereafter, Miss Harter came in again and, as usual, by her acts, words, and the tones of her voice tried to make herself as enticing as she could. She coyly offered me a suggestive picture for my private office, and she took the liberty of hanging it on my wall. I smiled and pretended to be pleased, thanked her, and kept on playing innocent and gullible. This led her to believe that she had me enchanted and within her power, no doubt to her great professional satisfaction. But as soon as she left, I took the picture down and immediately took it to two loyal nearby friends, Dr. and Mrs. Byers. I had them make faint secret marks and write the date and hour on the back of the picture. Of course I explained to them what was going on. Then I took the picture back to my office and hung it up where she had placed it so that no suspicion would likely be raised when she came in again.

About two hours later I had two visitors, Adams and Gilson, her two co-detectives, who had never been in my office before and had no business with me on this occasion. They explained that they just wanted to say "hello" and to see how I was getting along. They acted very friendly with me. After visiting a little while, Adams pretended to casually notice the picture, which seemed to intrigue him, and he stepped over to examine it. I could see that he was pleased that the evident report of his female conspirator was correct: that she had, in fact, presented me with this suggestive picture and that I kept it hanging on the wall of my private office. Adams made quite a fuss about the picture and asked me where I got it.

"Well," I said, with a sheepish look, "a lady friend gave it to me."

That was the answer they wanted so that they could report apparent progress to the Boss, that the chain of evidential facts to bind me was being successfully forged. The report would make the Boss feel that all was well and that he would soon get results for his money. Their long-range purpose was, of course, to entangle me so deeply and in such a manner that if I should ever claim that their activities were all part of a blackmailing effort of which I was at the time fully aware, they could rebut my claim. They would show that I had accepted a picture from this woman and kept it hanging in my office. By anticipating their scheme with the deeper plan

11

of having the picture marked by Dr. and Mrs. Byers I was in a position to thwart any possible claim they could make that I had suddenly set up the excuse of knowing about the scheme only after I had been trapped.

Then this brazen female again visited my office. After going through her usual acts of enticement and, of course, begging my pardon for being so forward, pouring out all sorts of compliments designed to intoxicate me and explaining how irresistible I was, to the extent of making her lose her head and dignity, she stated in a soft and timid voice that she had purchased two steamship tickets for a moonlight trip. She showed me the tickets and handed them to me. Of course I knew what she meant—that these tickets were for her and me—but I pretended to not understand. I thanked her for her kindness and said, "My wife and I will surely enjoy this trip."

She looked at me coyly and said, "Oh, I thought you understood that I meant them for you and me."

I handed the tickets back to her, feigning reluctance, and said, "Well, I'm sorry, but that's impossible." I then drolly explained, in a Will Rogers fashion, that I was a married man and had a family and wouldn't dare accept such an invitation—all of which, she, of course, well knew.

She said, "Oh, I thought you were wise and too broad-minded to have such narrow ideas."

While I continued to pretend to feel complimented, I also continued to decline as gracefully as I could without appearing the least bit insulted. When at last she left, I am sure she had the impression, which I intended her to have, that I was an old-fashioned conventionalist. But since my response appeared to be halfhearted, she probably felt she could still entangle me.

Luckily, it so happened that before this visit she had called me on the telephone and made an appointment. That gave me time to arrange for a male stenographer to be secreted within hearing distance. I had planned for such an emergency by stretching a large curtain across the corner in the rear of the large reception room. The curtain was behind a large folding mirror that was, with wings extended, eight feet wide and six feet high. This room arrangement looked quite natural, so no suspicions were aroused. Behind the curtain I had placed a small desk with pad and pencil. I always had this stenographer secreted there when I knew in advance of the coming of this would-be siren.

The steamship tickets of course had been paid for by the Boss in the hope of catching me in violation of the federal law against transporting a woman of Miss Harter's kind from one state to another. The penalty for such offense was a $5,000 fine and five years in the penitentiary. The Boss evidently figured that with such a penalty staring me in the face, I would be willing to settle for dismissal of the pending court actions.

A few days after the incident with the steamship tickets took place, my detective informed me that my client, Mrs. Mills, had been trapped. He told me how this female detective had inveigled Mrs. Mills into accepting an invitation to go to a neighboring city with her on an interurban railcar, at her expense; that after they had boarded the car, they just coincidentally happened to meet two men, apparently friends of Miss Harter. She introduced Adams and Gilson to Mrs. Mills. They became quite friendly, chatting, telling stories, and laughing all the way over. On nearing their destination, the men generously invited the ladies to have dinner with them. When the car stopped near a certain hotel the party of four got off and went to the hotel for dinner. Drinks were served with the dinner. Mrs. Mills was induced to drink a special green-colored drink, which my detective told me was spiked with absinthe. After dinner the four went upstairs and paired off, Gilson taking Mrs. Mills to one room with Adams and Miss Harter going to another adjoining room. There were two men already secreted in the adjoining room where Adams and Miss Harter went—the Boss and one of his attorneys. They were there to listen, but whether they had any special listening devices or a dictaphone arranged my detective was not sure. The parties remained in their respective rooms for an hour or so, coming out about the same time and meeting in the lobby. The party then broke up, and the women returned home by themselves.

When I learned these shocking facts the next day, I realized that Mrs. Mills's libel suit was practically finished. Now she would not dare to come into court. But I said nothing to her at the time—it was too late. I kept on playing "dumb" and biding my time in the hope of being able to successfully prosecute these culprits on a serious charge. I would thus end their vicious attempts to blackmail other gullible victims.

The culprits carried on with their deeply laid

scheme for about eight weeks. I then learned from my detective that the Boss was getting somewhat worried about having all their salaries and expenses to pay while seemingly getting no results with me. Entangling me was much more important to the Boss than merely trapping one of my clients. If he could silence me, the one pesky lawyer who was not afraid to file a suit against him or his newspaper, then other potential actions would never be started.

The Boss was beginning to insist on action and results from his hirelings. I learned that besides all expenses and salaries, he had offered a $500 bonus to each one of the three detectives if and when the scheme of trapping me proved successful.

Then one morning I was standing in front of my office on Main Street talking to a senior student of our local college, Mr. Evans. Miss Harter came along and asked me, in his presence, if she could see me at once in my office, which was on the second floor. I said, "Surely. Go on up and I will be up in a few minutes."

Again I had to think fast. I said to this student, "I want you to do me a favor. That woman is trying to blackmail me and I do not want to be alone with her." I told him that I would explain later, but just then I wanted him to go up to my office with me and listen to everything that was said. You see, I did not have time to contact and secrete my usual stenographer.

When we walked into the office she seemed surprised that I was not alone and excused herself and asked if she could see me at 3:30 that afternoon—"if that would be convenient."

I said, "Sure."

After she left, I explained the situation to Mr. Evans. I told him to remember the occasion and what had been said, as I probably would call on him later as a witness.

In the subsequent legal procedure I did call on him and he corroborated my statement in every detail. This was very important, as Miss Harter, after arrest, claimed she did not see me and was not in my office on the day in question. It was shown conclusively that she was there twice on that day.

Promptly at 3:30 that afternoon she came in, and apparently I was alone—just what she wanted. But I was not alone, for my stenographer was hidden behind the curtain where he could plainly hear everything that was said. Miss Harter sat down and went into her act of playing up to me, saying her usual nice things about me, what a wonderful fellow I was, etc. It still gives me pain to recall her hypocrisy. Then she said she would like very much to spend one evening alone with me before leaving the city, as she was intending soon. She said she had changed her rooming place and was now living on Market Street. The room that she had was on the ground floor, and it was so situated that it would be very convenient to have me visit her there. We would be alone—no one else would be in the house. She pictured this situation as an ideal rendezvous for her purpose, playing "a Delilah act." Again it was difficult for me to restrain my temper. I pretended to be pleased by her hypocritical flattery, but I guarded my words as best I could. My diplomacy was essential for keeping my own plans.

Finally she arose and was about to leave when in came a man, Mr. Waltman. Then she said to me so that he could hear, "So I'll see you tonight, then, at eight o'clock?"

I said, "OK" or something to that effect. She went out smiling, no doubt with an inward feeling of professional success. As soon as she had gone I said to Mr. Waltman, "You see that woman in here and heard what she said. Notice that clock. It is just twenty minutes to four, and don't you ever forget it in any court."

Then I walked over by the curtain behind which was the stenographer with his notebook, and quickly pulling the curtain aside, I said, "Now, Mr. Waltman, you see this stenographer and I want you to remember that also; and if you are called into court to testify about this matter, I'll expect you to tell these things exactly as they are."

Mr. Waltman looked surprised and quietly walked out of the office without saying a word. I doubt that he was in on the conspiracy, but no doubt was procured to be there exactly at 3:40 to hear the last words of our conversation about the rendezvous set for eight o'clock that evening—and, if ever necessary, to be available as a witness against me.

I knew that Mr. Waltman would make immediate report of this climax to those who had sent him to be there at the proper psychological moment. I also knew that the time had come for quick action. The conspirators would now learn that I was wise to their damnable racket. Although I was not quite ready to act, as I lacked proper evidence to land one or more of these conspirators in the penitentiary, I felt I did have sufficient grounds to arrest Miss Harter for the minor offense of disorderly conduct. The arrest would at least give me an opportunity to show the public the diabolical plot in the making. That was what I really wanted, for I felt that a public exposure would put an end to such blackmailing schemes in our community.

It was getting toward evening and the court would soon be closed. So I immediately drew up an affidavit charging the woman with disorderly conduct by way of attempting to carry out a blackmailing scheme. While I had never heard of anything exactly like this, I reasoned that any and all conduct was either orderly or disorderly, and her conduct certainly had not been orderly. The affidavit, leaving off formal parts, charged the woman who called herself Helen Harter, in substance:

> That she did unlawfully and contrary to the Ordinance of said city, violate the peace and good order of said city by indecent and disorderly conduct in planning, scheming and trying to wreck affiant's home, and proposing to affiant to spend an evening together in a house in said city, and making other and like proposals in a black-mailing scheme.

A warrant was accordingly issued for her arrest and placed in the hands of a trusted police officer with instructions to listen and find out whom she called, if anyone, when arrested. There were no dial phones in those days, so the police officer heard when she asked the operator for a number, which was later determined to be that of the residence phone of one of the attorneys for the newspaper in the libel suits. The police officer heard her say through the phone, "Then you say I should deny being in his office today. All right."

I also asked the arresting officer to let me know as soon as she was arrested and brought in to police headquarters, regardless of the time of night. About ten o'clock I was called and I went there immediately. There she was with about fifteen police officers gathered around to see the show.

As soon as I walked in, she stared daggers at me and said, "What in the hell is the matter with you, Mr. Emmons? Are you crazy? You know I wasn't even in your office today. I'll make you pay for this."

I sort of smiled and said, "Now, Miss Harter—but that isn't your name—stop your acting. It will do you no good. I know all about you and

21

the damnable business you are in. You ought to be ashamed, but the ones in back of you are even worse. You have no ill feeling toward me, but for a few dollars you would blackmail and ruin me and my family for the man who is paying you. I know who he is and how much you are getting a week and the bonus offered if you succeeded in trapping me. I know the attorney you called this evening and who will be one of the attorneys to defend you. But it will do you no good. You are caught in this blackmailing scheme to trap me, so you may as well tell the truth."

Then she calmed down, simply smiled, but said nothing more than to repeat time and again that she hadn't seen or been in my office that day.

When her case came on for trial she was represented not only by the two attorneys who were defending in the libel suits then pending, but also by two other attorneys. I had subpoenas issued for a number of witnesses, including the Boss and the two men detectives. But evidently they all had been warned about the subpoenas, and they evaded service. In fact, they got out of the city and stayed out until the case was over. Do you wonder why?

I also subpoenaed my client, the already-trapped Mrs. Mills. As soon as she got the subpoena she came in to see me. She wanted to know why she had been subpoenaed. I told her I wanted her to testify about her trip with Miss Harter and the two men on an interurban railcar to a neighboring city. At first she pretended not to know what I was talking about. But when I related the details of the trip, the dinner, the peculiar green drink, the pairing off, she and her new friend Gilson going to one room and Miss Harter and her friend Adams going to an adjoining room, she grew pale, and stared at me in great distress. Tears ran down her cheeks, and she threw up her hands and cried out, "Oh, my God, how did you find out all those things?"

I said, "They're true, aren't they?"

She replied, "Yes, but I didn't know anything about those people being there, and I'll not testify at all."

I asked, "Why not?"

Then she said, "Good heavens, my husband will kill me, and I know nothing about anyone else being in that room except Miss Harter and Adams."

Then I told her I would see her husband and frankly explain to him all the facts concerning the blackmailing scheme. I would point out that she had simply been the victim of a vicious plot to force them to drop their lawsuits against the Boss's newspaper. I stated further that after her husband learned these sordid facts he would not blame her or kill her, but, I added, "He might kill some others and I wouldn't blame him much if he did."

Mrs. Mills told me that she had never before tasted anything like this green drink; that it made her feel queer and that she did not realize what she was doing when she went into that room. She asserted with emphasis that she had not been guilty of any immoral conduct. I realized that her claim in that regard would likely be disputed, and so far as her libel suit was concerned, it was a hopeless case—guilty or not guilty—as I well knew the presumptions of law in such matters.

However, I wanted her as a witness, not for the purpose of directly showing what Miss Harter had done concerning myself as an attorney, on a particular day, but to show the wide scope of the conspiracy.

When the case came up for hearing, such a crowd had assembled that not one-fourth of the people could get into the fair-sized courtroom. Fortunately, the rival newspaper in our city carried the whole story with glaring headlines. At last the community learned to what lengths its political boss had gone in order to thwart and defeat legitimate lawsuits and maintain his and his newspaper's political prestige.

The defendant was found guilty, even though she had the benefit of four lawyers and the prestige of an influential newspaper. She was sentenced to pay a fine and costs. I had the feeling that my annoyances had not been in vain, as the thing I sought to accomplish had been accomplished. The people were awakened, and the prestige of this political boss and his newspaper was greatly depreciated. The regime of dictatorship in our city was ended.

The judgment of the court was appealed to a higher court of our county and was there affirmed.

Perhaps I should not have written this story, which—except for some of the names—is true in every detail. It all happened many years ago, yet it seems but yesterday to me. I was a young lawyer then, struggling for a foothold on the ladder to success in my profession. Mr. and Mrs. Mills were just ordinary young people, having the usual virtues and weaknesses. They had a legitimate claim for damages against a newspaper, which was defeated by high-handed and illegal methods. Because I had filed their respective claims in court against a political boss's newspaper, we—clients and their attorney—became the objects of a diabolical scheme to wreck our homes.

Chapter II
Murders, a Kidnapping, Etc.

While I faintly realized that I was taking on considerable responsibility in accepting the two libel lawsuits that led to exposing the damnable blackmailing plot, I did not contemplate getting involved so deeply. Before I knew it, I found myself championing the rights of not only the victims of this political boss, but also of the poor and weak in general. My sympathy always seemed to be for the underdog. I surely was not trying to play the reformer for glory, and it was not my intention or desire to get mixed up in trouble with the Boss and his newspaper. Nevertheless, the reaction that followed my efforts of exposure brought a favorable stimulus to my law business and put an end to the "starving period"

27

of my profession. I began to get all sorts of cases involving court proceedings from the lowest to the highest courts.

Without going into my general and more prosaic experiences, I will relate some other entanglements with the Boss that I encountered, scattered over a period of more than a decade.

As I went about my duties in civil and criminal matters in the various courts, this newspaper under the direction of the Boss purposely and deliberately kept my name out of its columns. Such a practice is known in the newspaper world as the "silent treatment," and it was applied to me in revenge. It was unethical for a lawyer to advertise, and this silent treatment amounted to a costly penalty in dollars and cents, to say nothing of its psychological and social effects. I will give one example in which the silent treatment was applied to me.

In a nearby village, a young girl died under such peculiar circumstances as to raise a strong suspicion that she had been murdered by her husband. Her father and sister thought so, and they employed an attorney to arrest the husband for murder. After arrest, the husband was brought before the village's mayor. The mayor dismissed the case, and the husband was set free.

The father and sister then sought my services. After being convinced that their suspicions were well founded, before the same court I had the man re-arrested for murder. This was an unusual action, and all the newspapers in the district played it up with headlines. The Boss's paper also made a great ado about the matter, with appropriate headlines, mentioning the attorneys for the defendant but never my name.

Due to my thorough investigation and presentation of further evidence, which I had unearthed and which had been purposely concealed, I was able to convince the mayor, who had previously dismissed the husband, that he should hold the defendant to the grand jury of the county. This he did. When I say "unearthed," I mean that both literally and figuratively, for the father and I dug to the bottom of a large ash pile in the defendant's backyard. There I found what I was looking for—a half-empty bottle of poison. The name of the poison, the drugstore, and date of sale were on the bottle's label. The drugstore had a record of the sale, and the clerk testified that he remembered selling it to the husband. The defendant was promptly indicted by the grand jury, and he was later convicted of the crime.

Thus through my efforts, a guilty man—a wife killer—was brought to justice for a heinous crime. And right to the end, the names of the attorneys for the defendant were given prominence in the Boss's newspaper, while I continued to get the silent treatment.

Sometime later, the same scandalmonger reporter referred to earlier in the blackmailing case wrote a fantastic, false, and malicious story involving a prominent woman of our city. We will call her Mrs. March. She called at my office and, after a long consultation, requested me to file a libel suit against the Boss's newspaper for damages to her good name and reputation. I doubt if any other lawyer in the district would have risked the enmity of this newspaper by accepting such a lawsuit, even if he believed the suit to be meritorious and justifiable. Their reluctance is cowardice, but I can't blame them too much. Lawyers have to make a living, too, and to stand in well with a newspaper is a great help.

I did not start my law career with the idea of fighting this newspaper or the Boss. But after the early blackmail case, I got to be known as a lawyer who would accept cases against this powerful boss and his press. I paid no attention to the poet's words: "Fools rush in where angels fear to tread"; instead I accepted this lady's case and filed her claim for damages. In due time the case was tried. In spite of the prestige and influence of this paper throughout the county, and the services of three attorneys, the jury rendered a substantial verdict for my client and against the newspaper.

On another occasion, based upon a slight suspicion, the Boss used his influence to cause the arrest of a hardworking man, whom we will call Mr. Jackson. The charge was fraud: purposeful miscounting of production in the Boss's small factory. There was no motive whatever for Mr. Jackson to miscount and register a larger production, since he was paid by the hour. At the hearing it was shown that the counting records probably had been stepped up secretly by another man who was being paid by the number and thus had a motive to overcount. The defendant was acquitted by the mayor in whose court the affidavit for arrest had been filed.

Mr. Jackson had a good reputation and had never been arrested or charged with any offense before in his life. He therefore rightfully felt he had been injured and was entitled to damages. He sought my services, and I filed a suit for him against the Boss for malicious prosecution.

When the case came to trial, the main defense set up by the Boss's attorney was, in substance, that Jackson had not yet been acquitted of the charge before the mayor. The defense claimed, according to the record of the mayor's court, the case was still pending and not yet disposed. Such a defense, if true, would absolutely defeat any malicious prosecution case, which I well knew. Was the defense claim true? It was not! Knowing this technicality in law, before filing the case for Mr. Jackson, I had gone to this mayor's office and examined the docket. The docket showed that the defendant had been dismissed and the case was ended. I made a copy of the record. The attorneys representing the Boss figured they had an ace witness that would dispose of the damage case very quickly, and they put on the witness stand the mayor, who was a friend of the Boss. The mayor testified that the criminal case had not been dismissed and produced the docket to corroborate his sworn statement. Knowing what the defense was going to be, I had brought into court a magnifying glass. On cross-examination of the mayor, I handed him the magnifying glass, asking him to use it and tell the court and jury what entry, if any, had been made before the one now found on the record. He saw the point, realizing its purport and the danger of testifying to a falsehood. Therefore, he admitted to the court and jury that he had changed the record after the damage case had been filed by attempting to erase the former record of "case dismissed" and write over it the words "case continued." Do you wonder whose influence caused the mayor to change the record?

At the close of several days' trial and arguments of counsel for the respective parties, the case was submitted to the jury. I was quite wrought up about the unsavory tactics used by opposing counsel, and in the most caustic language I was able to command, I charged the Boss with misconduct in causing court records to be changed and stated that such a man should be in the penitentiary.

After the judge had charged the jury and it had gone out to the jury room for deliberation, I started to leave the courtroom for a breath of fresh air. The Boss motioned to me and asked me to sit down beside him. Was I surprised! He began a friendly conversation. He said he would like it if some understanding could be reached whereby our relationship would be on a friendlier basis, as he thought that would be of mutual benefit. I told him that I would do my part to bring about such a condition. In brief, we did, then and there, while the jury was out, come to an understanding about any future controversies. He was to give me fair and full consideration in his newspaper columns, and I would not thereafter file any lawsuit against him or his newspaper without first making a strenuous effort to get it adjusted on some reasonable basis. Of course such an understanding would be of mutual benefit, and no third party's interest would be jeopardized.

After an hour or two of deliberation in the jury room, the jury returned to the courtroom and announced a verdict in favor of my client. The amount was for a substantial amount against the Boss, which he later paid in full.

I had no occasion to file another lawsuit against the Boss or his newspaper for quite a while. The newspaper and the Boss seemed to be on their good behavior, so far as I was concerned. Then one day a new mayor of our city, Mr. Wallace, came into my office. I had been his campaign manager when he was running for office, and I wrote all of his campaign literature and advertising matter. One item was a twenty-page booklet of which 10,000 copies were printed and distributed. In this booklet I endeavored to show the connection between certain influential people, including politicians, and corporations that were opposing Mr. Wallace's election and the motive and purpose behind their efforts. Mr. Wallace was elected in spite of the Boss's newspaper, which was against him from the beginning of the campaign and which used its full strength to defeat him. Mr. Wallace carried every precinct in the city.

Political conditions had changed in the intervening years, and were still changing. Naturally I had a feeling of satisfaction that I had helped bring about this change. Yet after this election, the Boss, through the columns of his paper, relentlessly criticized Mr. Wallace's administration. Of course, the Boss was within his legal rights so long as such criticisms were kept within bounds of reason and were based upon facts. However, the irresponsible reporter described before wrote a false, malicious, and damaging story about Mr. Wallace, charging him with corruption and being directly connected with the underworld. There was no basis for such charges!

When he came to me, the mayor explained that he was there for advice and immediate legal action against this newspaper; that he felt ruined and had been made quite ill and had needed to consult a doctor. He pulled down his shirt and showed me how his skin had acquired rashes all over his body. He said his doctor told him it came from nervousness brought about by worry over this attack on his character. I went over the matter very carefully with him and told him that, in my opinion, he had a very good libel case. But because of my "gentleman's agreement" with the Boss, which I explained, I would like to excuse myself from accepting his case. He said he understood and then asked if I would give him private aid in the matter, which I then promised.

I explained to Mr. Wallace that I believed this newspaper still had too much influence with the courts and juries of this county because of its wide general circulation. After thinking over the possibilities for a few minutes, I asked him to wait until I had investigated the idea of filing his claim in another county. After checking on the law so far as I could in a short time, I came to the conclusion that the venue of the case could be changed, and I worked out a plan whereby it could be filed in the adjoining county, where the Boss and his newspaper would have little influence. So I advised Mr. Wallace accordingly and explained exactly how it could be done. I knew the Boss was president and manager of a small manufacturing company located in the adjacent county. I instructed the mayor that he should file his case through a certain attorney of that county whom I recommended. I detailed the procedure: that the suit should be filed about 3:00 P.M. on a particular day when the Boss was at his factory (if the suit was filed before that time, news dispatches to his paper would warn him and he could evade service by merely staying out of that county) and a deputy sheriff should make special service on the Boss in his capacity as president of the newspaper corporation as soon after filing as the deputy could drive to the factory. I also gave my opinion that if the Boss were served personally, the service would be valid and would bring this newspaper within the jurisdiction of the other county's courts.

Mr. Wallace then consulted confidentially with another attorney who gave an opposing opinion that such service would be improper on the nonresident newspaper corporation. However, the mayor took my advice, believing that his only hope for justice was to get his case out of the county. He then obtained assistance from the attorney I recommended. The case was filed exactly as I had outlined, and the Boss was served. Attorneys for the Boss evidently regarded it as a joke, claiming that the summons was illegal and not binding on the nonresident corporation. Therefore, they filed a motion to dismiss and demurrer, setting up their theory of the law in the proper legal manner to test such a technicality. But the court and higher courts sustained my theory, and the case came on for trial. It was strenuously fought, and the jury returned a verdict of $23,500 against the newspaper. This was the highest verdict ever rendered in a libel suit against a newspaper in our state, up to that time.

Following this case and verdict, I believe this newspaper really tried to be careful and ethical. Citizens' reputations and characters were guarded more closely and held considerably more sacred than formerly. Perhaps the Boss did some thinking and came to realize that while he might not understand it, juries evidently had faith in Shakespeare's words:

> Who steals my purse steals trash;
> But he that filches from me my good name
> Robs me of that which not enriches him
> And makes me poor indeed.

The Boss might have remembered, too, the words of the Bible:

A good name is rather to be chosen than great riches.

In any event, I do not believe it is incorrect for me to claim some little credit for this wholesome reformation, which was a plainly discernible benefit to the community.

Nothing of particular interest to the public happened thereafter as concerned the Boss, his newspaper, and myself for several years.

Then one day a woman whom I did not know, whom I will call Mrs. Ross, walked into my office and introduced herself. She said the reason she had come to see me was because she had been present in the big crowd that attended the trial of Helen Harter for disorderly conduct in the blackmailing scheme. She said she had heard the whole case and had liked the way I fought it against the four lawyers defending that woman. She then and there had made up her mind that if she ever needed a lawyer, she would come to me. She said that she had cried at that trial. I thanked her, of course, for the compliment and asked her what her present problem was. She stated that she felt her son, Webb Ross, eighteen years of age, was in deep trouble, the nature and details of which she did not understand. She wanted my help. I told her to have her son, Webb, and his father come in with her. I would try to determine the facts and see what, if anything, could be done.

At the appointed time all three came in, and I immediately went to work on this teenager, using all the psychology I knew, to get the whole truth from him, in the presence of his parents. The facts came out. It was a very serious matter. And it was startling! Young Webb was employed by one (I'll call him) Jim Carr, who was at that time a man of responsible standing in the community and, with his wife and family, a great church worker. Webb's parents had been induced by Carr to put practically all their savings into the purchase of stock in an interurban bus company, a corporation organized by Carr and of which he was president and manager. The corporation was not paying dividends, as promised by Carr, which worried the boy as well as his parents. At various times, and at psychological moments, Carr explained confidentially to Webb that the reason the company was not paying was because of unfair and prejudicial false articles about the bus company published in the Boss's newspaper. While there had been a few mild articles about this company in the paper criticizing the management, this excuse was largely false, but the boy fully believed Carr's story. Even the parents, when they first came into my office, believed these stories.

These trumped-up excuses told to Webb by Carr were intended to make Webb angry at the Boss. The boy was made to feel that the Boss was deliberately trying to ruin his parents, as well as endanger his own job, through wrecking the bus company. And Carr told him that after the bus company became bankrupt, the Boss was going to grab it and make money from it for himself. The boy was whipped into a frenzy about this alleged archenemy of himself and his parents. Carr showed Webb typewritten letters from the Boss, with his name affixed, threatening the ruination of the bus company. These letters were very convincing, as they came through the mail.

The boy and his parents, at the time these revelations were being made to me, implicitly believed the letters to be genuine. But I well knew that no matter what the Boss might have done in the past, he was not ignorant enough to write and sign threatening letters and send them through the mail.

Right here, let me note that the Boss was absolutely innocent of these charges, which had been deliberately concocted by Carr in order to manipulate young Webb. But to the boy the stories were real, and he was ready to do anything—yes, anything—to avenge these wrongs.

The actual fact was, as I then figured and afterward proved, that Carr had dissipated the bus company's money. After getting the boy in the proper mood for his purpose, Carr convinced Webb what needed to be done and that he wanted the boy's help. This was the plan: They would pretend to hitch a ride with the Boss on a certain evening about five o'clock when he would be going home from his office; they would then stick a gun into the Boss's ribs and force him to drive them out to an abandoned coal bank about ten miles out in the country; then they would make him write and sign a note to his wife, telling her strictly confidentially that he had gotten a young girl "in trouble" and was leaving for parts unknown until the trouble passed over, and not to worry about him, no matter how long he would be gone, as he would be all right; that she was to ask no questions of the bearer but get and give

42

him $20,000 in cash. This note was to be written and signed by the Boss at the point of a gun and was to be delivered by the boy, Webb. After the money was received by Carr, they would then kill the Boss and take his body back into the abandoned mine, where it would never be found. Quite a hellish scheme! But that was the plan, and it was almost fully carried out on the thirtieth day of June 1922.

On that day they did kidnap the Boss, as Carr planned, and forced him to drive out to the coal bank. There he pleaded for his life for six hours, but was finally able to talk them into trusting him to pay the $20,000 cash on the next day if they would release him. Otherwise they would get nothing, for he refused to write and sign such a note to his wife even if they would kill him. They then released him and told him it would cost him his life if he breathed a word of this to anyone. Jim Carr was to call at the Boss's office the next day and get the money.

He did call. The Boss got him into his private office and told him all the cash he could possibly raise at that time was $6,000. This amount he gave to Carr, promising to pay the balance agreed upon in a day or two. No other money was ever paid, but Carr warned him that if he failed to pay, it would cost him his life. The Boss had a Dicta-phone secreted and witnesses listening but, nev-ertheless, was afraid to have Carr arrested for fear it would cost him his life. The Boss felt that his evidence would be insufficient to obtain a conviction of the kidnappers and would-be mur-derers. The Boss became very ill from shock and worry; figuratively, he was almost scared to death.

The boy, Webb Ross, further explained how lately Carr had been trying to get him to help put the Boss out of the way for good, for as long as he was alive their liberty was at stake. Webb also told me that Carr had arranged for Webb to take a drive with him the next evening but had di-rected Webb to tell no one where he was going or whom he was going with. From many other things young Webb told me, it seemed clear that Carr was intending to get rid of the Boss and perhaps the boy, too. At least one of them would have to be liquidated. If either the Boss or Webb should come up missing, Carr could feel safe.

This whole kidnapping, robbery and at-tempted murder was kept absolutely secret when the $6,000 was paid, until it was confessed and detailed to me by this eighteen-year-old boy. I did some sober thinking. If this case were

44

sprung in a clumsy manner, it might cost the lives of the boy, the Boss, and even myself. I cautioned the boy and his parents not to tell another soul about the matter. Webb was definitely not to go out riding or to be alone with Carr until they heard from me.

Concerning this Jim Carr, my memory began recalling some weird happenings of bygone days. My connection with the details seemed remarkably coincidental, making me almost believe that a Divine Hand had steered information about certain crimes across my pathway for a purpose.

Many years before this kidnapping, I was consulted and given information by a thoroughly reliable person that this same Jim Carr, with whom I was not acquainted at the time, had committed a murder. For fear of involving two innocent persons now living who knew of the murder but kept publicly silent, I will not elaborate further. But the motive, means, and facts of that murder were quite conclusive.

Again, four or five years after that murder, Jim Carr came into my office, introduced himself, and explained that he had been arrested falsely on suspicion of murdering a policeman in another city. A policeman had been killed in a battle with a robber before daylight that very morning. Carr said he knew nothing about the murder and that he had no connection with it. He further explained that on that particular morning he had taken a train; that as his train made a scheduled stop about twenty miles away, two plainclothes police officers boarded the train and came into his coach. One sat down directly behind him, and the other squatted down beside him and immediately stuck a gun in his ribs so hard that it punctured and injured his side and made him suffer severe pain. They informed him that he was under arrest for murder, and they took him away from the train and placed him in jail.

The officers, no doubt, acted in good faith, because Carr answered the description of the murderer given by the dying policeman. When Carr was brought before the mayor for a hearing, he explained who he was—that he was a businessman—and the mayor dismissed the charge. Carr's reactions to the whole proceeding seemed natural; he was wrought up and angry for being in jail and for such rough usage. I, like the mayor, thought he was innocent, and in accordance with Carr's instruction I prepared a wrongful arrest case against these two officers and their city, asking for $25,000 damages.

When he came back to my office a few days later to sign the papers, I asked him to open his shirt and show me the injury that he claimed was likely to be permanent. But he made some excuse and said he would be in again in a few days. When he did return, I asked him to show me the wound or scar, but again he would not comply, saying that it wasn't necessary. At the time I thought he had been exaggerating his injury and was ashamed to have let me catch him in a falsehood. But he also seemed to have lost interest in pursuing the matter, and so I dropped the case. Many years had to pass before I was able to understand why he didn't want me to see the wound. You see, the dying policeman had not only given a description of his murderer, but had said that he thought he had shot the murderer as he fled.

Memory also recalled to me that at the time Carr organized the bus company another mysterious episode occurred. A wealthy man from an eastern state had come to our city with $20,000 in cash with the purpose of investing it in this bus company. His trip was in accordance with an understanding reached through correspondence with Jim Carr. According to the man's relatives, he had the cash when he left home, he had arrived, and he had met with Carr. The wealthy man had not returned home, and relatives had received no word from him. In spite of thorough tracing efforts no further information of this man's whereabouts was ever found.

With these historical facts and the evidently truthful story told me by the boy, I had little difficulty in believing the fantastic and sensational kidnapping story and that Carr planned another murder. I could believe this of Carr, although at that time Carr stood high in the community. He was a generous supporter of his church, and its minister, Reverend Ramsey, was a close friend.

After full consideration I got busy. I realized that both the boy's life and the Boss's life were in danger. I telephoned the Boss and asked him to come to my office. I told him it was important, but I gave no hint of what I wanted. He came at the appointed time, and I was alone.

I said, "Fred, on last June 30, you were kidnapped—" but I didn't get any further.

He jumped up like a rabbit and, as though he had been shot, turned pale and said, "My God, Emmons, are you also in with that gang?"

I said calmly, "No, Fred, I am not in the gang and I only want to save your life, and possibly the life of a young man, and I want to put the criminal behind bars."

He trembled all over at first and seemed to be very afraid of me. I assured him again and again that my motives were the best and that it would be to his interest to cooperate.

"But," he said, "I cannot prove Carr kidnapped me, and my life is at stake. What do I care about the $6,000 I paid when my life is at stake?"

Finally I convinced him that he must act; that he was in more danger if he were not to act. I assured him that with his cooperation we could land Carr in the penitentiary, where he deserved to be. I explained to him how young Webb was inveigled into helping his employer commit this crime and that, under my advice, Webb would tell the whole story when and where we wanted him to. I also explained the danger Webb was in and my feelings of duty toward him and his parents, who had employed me. I asked the Boss's cooperation in saving this boy from penalty, as he was unknowingly led into this dastardly scheme by lies, forged letters, etc. The Boss thanked me over and over again as he came to understand my intentions and plans. He promised his full cooperation. As he was leaving my office, he told me that he felt better than he had at any time since the kidnapping. He said he now had hope for a solution.

I caused an affidavit to be filed, a warrant issued, and under my supervision, at the proper psychological moment, had the defendant followed and arrested in a hotel in another city. There Carr—this good church member—was registered with his secretary under assumed names as husband and wife.

He was brought back to our city. I suggested to the officers that when he was brought in, they should question him on other troubles he had been into and at the right moment tear open his shirt to see if there were any scars on his side. Doing this, they found a deep scar on one side, apparently made by a bullet. When they asked him about it, he told them what he had told me—that it had been made by the end of a policeman's revolver pressed against him so hard that it penetrated his skin and injured his rib. But I had no doubt that the scar had been made at the scene of the robbery by the bullet fired by the murdered policeman.

The arrest of Carr, this prominent business-man, on a sensational kidnapping and robbery charge, caused big headlines throughout the country and especially in our state. Therefore, when the preliminary hearing came up to be heard in a few days, the large municipal courtroom and adjoining rooms and hallways were packed with spectators, including newspaper reporters, court attachés, and attorneys. Carr was represented by a well-known attorney who was paid $250 per day by Carr's father.

The first move in the hearing was made as this attorney filed a motion to dismiss the action, based on some minor clerical error in the record. To the surprise of almost everyone, this big high-powered attorney, with a thunderous voice and aggressive attitude, bluffed the municipal judge into sustaining this motion. The judge dismissed the action for technical reasons that had nothing to do with the merits of the case. And when I say "bluffed," I mean that literally. There was no valid legal justification for sustaining the motion. The defendant, however, was immediately re-arrested before he left the courtroom on the same charges, but with the alleged clerical errors corrected. The hearing then proceeded, and at its conclusion the court bound the defendant over to the grand jury under a very heavy bond.

The day after the Municipal Court had sustained the motion to dismiss, the defendant, through his attorney, filed a suit against the Boss for $100,000 for malicious prosecution. This was just another bluff on the part of this attorney. He well knew, as any attorney well knows, that no malicious prosecution action such as his can be maintained successfully in any court, unless the case is dismissed or finally concluded in favor of the defendant. This sort of bluffing is what is known in law as a frivolous action. The action is not being filed in good faith but rather for propaganda purposes. Its aim is to plant seeds of doubt in the minds of the public and possibly prejudice prospective jurors.

In due time this frivolous suit was dismissed by the court at plaintiff's costs. But in the interim, while this suit was pending, the defendant had a right to take depositions of any witnesses he might desire to call.

In a few days after the fictitious damage suit had been filed, the attorney for Carr had subpoenas issued for taking of depositions of three witnesses who were to appear at a certain time and place, before a justice of the peace. The three witnesses were my clients, Mr. and Mrs. Ross and their son, Webb, who had accompanied Carr in perpetrating the crime. The procedure of taking depositions is often indulged in, but sometimes simply as "fishing expeditions" to find out in advance what adverse parties or witnesses may say when the actual case is called for trial. Depositions are not affidavits. An affidavit may be taken privately at any time, while depositions are allowed to be taken under authority and within the jurisdiction of the court in which the legal action is pending. But reasonable notice must be given to adverse party who may be there and cross-examine the witnesses. The evidence so taken may be used in the trial of the action in the court. A notary public or a justice of the peace before whom such depositions are taken is given the same authority as a judge of a court to compel attendance, exclude witnesses at the hearing before giving their testimony, and compel witnesses to answer any proper questions asked. And the justice of the peace or notary can punish for contempt for not obeying any legal order or ruling laid down by this magistrate, on the same basis as any court.

The kidnapping case and the frivolous action for malicious prosecution pending in the court had become quite notorious in our community. So the news about the taking of these depositions soon spread.

Therefore a crowd assembled in and around the large offices of this justice of the peace, who was also a lawyer and who will be referred to hereafter as "the Squire." When both sides to the controversy were ready, Carr's lawyer moved that these three witnesses be excluded until called, and the motion was sustained without objection. This attorney then called Mr. and Mrs. Ross to give their respective testimonies. Although the attorney was shrewd and asked many leading and catch questions, these witnesses answered promptly, but they knew no facts. After they had given their testimony and had been cross-examined and excused from further testimony, I motioned them to sit down near me in the courtroom, which they did. I wanted these parents near me when their son was called for examination, which was to follow immediately. Carr's attorney objected and asked the Squire to exclude them from the courtroom while their son's evidence was being taken. I stated that they should be permitted to stay for the reason that they had already testified and had been excused; the court had no right to further exclude them, as this was a public hearing. I further insisted that they owed it to their minor son, and to me as his counsel, to be immediately available for possible assistance in the serious matter involving their son. But the Squire ordered them to leave, which they refused to do. The controversy between adverse counsel and myself waxed hot. Many sharp words passed between us, each claiming that the other was trying to impose his will on the court. In the midst of this altercation, Mr. Ross jumped to his feet and said, "I am an American citizen, a taxpayer, and I'm going to stay in this courtroom," and he defied anyone to try to put him or his wife out.

But the Squire ordered the constable to remove Mr. and Mrs. Ross from the courtroom. When the constable came to do so, I jumped up and told the court and the constable that, in my opinion, the order was unreasonable and illegal and could not be legally enforced. The constable then refused to enforce the order, to my delight and the visible dissatisfaction of opposing counsel.

Then young Webb was called as a witness. I had already privately instructed him the day before not to answer any question at this hearing pertaining to the kidnapping and robbery episode. I explained to him that, under the Constitution of the United States, he would not be required to do so. I also explained to him, of course, that he should answer other questions that might be asked of him. However, no matter what happened, he should refuse to answer any questions for which his answers would tend to be incriminating. He promised to obey my instructions explicitly. So when opposing counsel, after some introductory questions concerning Webb's name, address, age, etc., started to ask him questions concerning the kidnapping and robbery episode, he refused to answer, stating his constitutional rights and that he had been advised by his counsel to refuse to answer any such questions. This made Carr's attorney furious at the witness, as well as at myself. He said many unkind things, about me as a lawyer for handing out such advice and about the witness for being such a fool as to take such advice, etc. He even demanded that the Squire put me in jail for contempt of court.

Naturally, I also got heated up at counsel's belligerent attitude, and I severely criticized him and his conduct in this and other courts that I knew about. In the heat of this verbal battle, I said that he ought to be ashamed of himself for charging the father of his client, who had employed him, $250 a day without rendering worthwhile service. As he had criticized me very severely and poked fun at the kind of advice I had given, I replied that when the last chapter of the case was written, the clients and public would know which lawyer had given the most effective service to his client. I declared that I was willing to risk my reputation as a lawyer in predicting that when this last chapter was written, my client, Webb Ross, would go free and his client would find himself in the penitentiary with a number on his back. This further infuriated him, drove him quite mad, and judging from his looks and actions he had a strong urge to strike me with his fists. He was a much larger man than I, but I refused to be bluffed, even though I knew that on a previous occasion he had actually assaulted another attorney in a courtroom. I felt that he might beat me, but he couldn't bluff me.

All of these proceedings were being taken down by two stenographers. After the melee, the Squire ruled that Webb had to answer the questions. But under my advice the witness still refused to answer any and all questions regarding the kidnapping and robbery, regardless of the threat by the Squire to imprison him. Adverse counsel then threatened that he was going to make Webb answer the questions if it took a week. I replied that he was not going to answer the questions regardless of how long the lawyer might continue to ask them. However, I also explained to the court that at the right time and proper place, my client would be willing to tell all he knew about these matters. Carr's counsel then jumped to his feet, pawed the air with his arms, strutted around, and banged the desk with his fists and demanded that the Squire find the witness and myself both guilty of contempt of court and send us to jail. I promptly challenged the court to do this and stood squarely on constitutional rights—and with full faith in Shakespeare's words, "Thrice is he arm'd that hath his quarrel just."

The court sided with opposing counsel and, with his assistance, made a finding of contempt and issued an order that the witness be placed in the county jail for ten days. The justice handed this order, which had been meticulously made with the assistance of opposing counsel, to the constable for execution. Then I jumped to my feet and warned the constable that if he took the witness to jail under such an order, which in my opinion was wholly illegal, null and void, he and his bondsman would be immediately sued for $10,000 damages for false imprisonment. The constable knew that I meant it and was scared enough to refuse to carry out the order. Then opposing counsel insisted that the Squire call the chief of police and get him to carry out the order. The chief was called. He came over to the courtroom immediately, and the Squire officially deputized him to execute the sentence of imprisonment. I then warned the chief of the facts and the legal phases of the matter and that, in my opinion, this order was absolutely illegal, null and void; if he attempted to execute it, he and his bondsman would be sued for $10,000 damages. The chief was also scared enough to refuse to carry out the order, although he had been duly deputized to do so by the Squire.

In the meantime, while these arguments and controversies had been going on, the crowd had become greatly excited and apparently was enjoying the show in the highest degree. One of the spectators, Reverend Ramsey, was quite agitated and dissatisfied, and he made some rather uncomplimentary remarks about me. I simply replied, "Reverend, you don't know what you are talking about. You had better keep quiet until these matters are determined in court."

Finally, Carr's attorney insisted that the only thing left for the court to do was to telephone the county sheriff and get him or one of his deputies to carry out the order, as provided by law when a constable cannot or will not act.

Otherwise the witness and his counsel could continue to make fools of the court.

The Squire also was wrought up by the stinging remarks, and he was now bent on imprisoning this witness to save his own dignity. So he immediately telephoned the county sheriff and asked him to come or send a deputy to carry out his order. Before the Squire hung up the phone, I asked him to let me talk to the sheriff. I said that if he didn't, I would immediately place another call to the sheriff. So he allowed me to talk. I explained to the sheriff the facts and that the Squire's order involved the constitutional rights of a witness. The sheriff then said to me, "You just tell the Squire he should go to hell."

I turned around, in the presence of the whole room of spectators and opposing counsel, and said, in a clear, loud voice so everybody could hear, "Squire, the sheriff told me to tell you to go to hell."

That was too much for the crowd. The people couldn't control themselves any longer! They stomped their feet, they clapped their hands, and they whistled with delight—to my full satisfaction and the very evident mental suffering of my opponent. My client was asked no more questions, and the depositions ended there. The "fishing expedition" was a flop.

The next day, someone anonymously left a box of fine cigars at my office, with a complimentary note enclosed. I never knew where they came from.

Perhaps you may wonder why I was so determined and insistent that Webb Ross's testimony not be given in the frivolous civil suit, as demanded by opposing counsel. I had several reasons, but the main one was that I did not want to endanger my changes of being able to plea-bargain with the prosecutor in the criminal cases. Otherwise I would not be doing my duty to my client. I wanted to hold the key to his liberty.

The grand jury indicted both of the participants in the kidnapping—the boy, Webb Ross, as well as Jim Carr. However, I held the key for either acquittal or conviction of Carr. Knowing and explaining the facts to the prosecutor I came to a "gentleman's understanding" with him, which under statutory regulations we had a right to do.

Remember that under the Constitution of the United States, no defendant or witness need testify about anything that might incriminate himself. So if I advised my client Webb, the boy, to refuse to testify, Carr, the real criminal, probably would go free. With the understanding that my client would not be prosecuted and the case against him would be dismissed if he came forward and helped the prosecution, I advised Webb to tell the whole story in court, from the beginning to end, including the typewritten letters alleged to have been signed by the Boss, and which I had felt from the beginning had been written on Carr's own typewriter.

I spent some time and effort in locating this typewriter, which Carr had owned about the time the letters were written. I found it had been sold to a student of our local college and later taken by him to Baltimore, Maryland. I went to Baltimore and located and got acquainted with the young man who had purchased the typewriter "for a song." This young man turned out to be a member of my own college fraternity, and he was very cooperative. I explained to him the purpose of my visit and that it was necessary to have this typewriter in court to determine whether or not certain threatening letters had been written on it. I got his promise to give me full cooperation. When the time came, he brought the machine into court, and it was proven by experts, using microscopes and photography, that the letters in question had been written on this very type-writer. It was valuable evidence.

The trial was a long one. The defendant was represented by a high-powered lawyer from a big city. But Carr was found guilty and sentenced to the state penitentiary for a term of from seven to thirty years. Later the indictment against my client Webb Ross was dismissed.

After Carr had been incarcerated in the penitentiary about eight years, he made application for parole. An investigator from the state capital came to see me. By this time in my career, I had moved to a larger city and was the city's safety director—head of the Police and Fire Departments, which included about two hundred men. The investigator sought me out to learn all I could tell him about Carr. I told him all I knew, including details of the three probable murders earlier related. He was amazed at the story and was intrigued by the coincidence of the gruesome facts crossing my pathway. Then he asked me what I thought ought to be done with the application for parole. I told him emphatically that it should be rejected, explaining that Carr had a dual personality—was a real Dr. Jekyll and Mr. Hyde. I made the remark that had I been his lawyer, I would not have denied any of the charges made, as denial caused a long-drawn-out lawsuit costing Carr's father $250 a day. Instead I would have had him plead insanity, which would have kept him in the State Institution for the Criminally Insane for many years. Although I did not recommend that at this late date he should be so committed, the investigator went back to the state capital and recommended that Carr be sent to the institution. This was accordingly done.

From my study of sociology and psychology, and after many years in the practice of law, I can say with conviction that we have too many soft but well-intentioned officers—judges, juries, and parole boards. At the institution this dangerous man was allowed privileges and some freedom. Thus given the opportunity, Carr escaped, endangering the lives of all of us who were responsible for his conviction, as well as any innocent person who might cross his path. Of course, he was not a danger to the ones who were soft enough to give him the chance to escape.

As soon as I learned of his escape, I was worried, and I often carried a gun. I thought that Carr might come after me and try to kill me. Neither I nor anyone else in the area heard from Carr for a couple of years. Important unanswered questions stayed with me: Who was paying for the soft inefficiency of the institution? How did Carr subsist? How many people had he killed and robbed in those years? Later I found out that Carr had traveled all over the United States.

One evening he suddenly appeared at the residence of John Bond, one of the high officials of the National Bank. John knew him instantly but could do nothing about it except be diplomatic and keep his eyes and ears open. He even invited Carr to stay all night and offered him a bed. But Carr was too smart for that. He told John, "No, I'm going to sit up all night and you are going to stay with me, and don't you or your wife or your young daughter try any monkey business. Your wife and daughter are going to bed." He emphasized the order by brandishing a gun.

When morning came, Carr ordered John to go down to his bank and get $50,000 and bring it back to him, and not to say a word to anyone; that he would hold his wife and daughter as hostages and if he tipped off the police they would pay with their lives. It was an awful dilemma John Bond found himself in. Personally, I think I would have gotten the money and done exactly as Carr ordered. But John did not do this. He went to the police!

Carr, in the meantime, had herded the wife and daughter upstairs. He stood downstairs by a large window, with a gun in his hand, watching and waiting. To the terrified wife and daughter it seemed like hours. After a while the wife heard some noises outside and then heard him say, "Here come the sons of bitches."

Then she heard a shot and the sound of a falling body just as the police and her husband rushed the house. Then she heard her husband's voice calling, and felt great relief to know that he was not injured. The shot she had heard was made by Carr's gun turned on himself. He had committed suicide. Her family was safe.

There are some other aspects of the kidnapping and robbery story that may be of interest. Although the Boss was the political boss of the town and virtual owner of its main newspaper, he was far from being personally popular. This was particularly true after the exposures I brought about. His unpopularity, I believe, was one reason why Jim Carr thought he might get away with the kidnapping and robbery. Perhaps in a showdown in court, the Boss's word would not be believed by the jurors. To emphasize the

Boss's unpopularity and make him still more unpopular was, no doubt, one of the reasons why Carr's attorney got permission from Reverend Ramsey and the trustees of the large church to which Carr belonged to let him take the pulpit. The plan was to have the defense attorney explain to the public that the defendant was innocent and that the Big Bad Wolf was about to eat one of its prominent members, a substantial citizen of their city.

They called the meeting and the church was packed to overflowing. Figuratively speaking, the whole town was there, including myself. Carr's lawyer appeared shrewd, magnetic, and convincing, just like most lawyers can be when only one side is presented. At this time probably he did believe that his client was an innocent victim. But the improper purpose of this church meeting was propaganda and an attempt to reach prospective jurymen and -women, directly or indirectly.

The next day the Boss called at my residence and asked for my advice. I told him that this church affair was something I had never heard of before and that no other lawyer had either! I hardly knew what to say. In the end I told him that the only thing to do was fight fire with fire, propaganda with propaganda; to make a demand in writing to Reverend Ramsey and each one of the church trustees to allow an attorney for the prosecuting witness the same privilege as was extended to the defendant's attorney. I also told the Boss to publish a copy of this request with big headlines on the first page of his paper. I predicted that Reverend Ramsey and the church trustees would not dare accept such a challenge. That would be fine. But if they did accept, that also would be fine!

The Boss left my house stating that he wanted to consult with other attorneys. About two hours later he returned and told me that the other attorneys had advised him that this would be foolish and of no value whatever.

"But," he added, "I decided to take your advice," and he showed me a copy of the demand and challenge he was putting in his newspaper, on top of the front page.

This demand and challenge did the trick. As I had predicted, the church refused to comply, and trouble and confusion ensued. Popular clamor, opinions, and sympathy in the city were noticeably neutralized. In general, the public was for fair play. There was the general feeling that a trial should be in a court of law and not in a church. The church was nearly wrecked by these unheard-of and ill-considered proceedings. Reverend Ramsey left the city soon after the court trial ended, with the conviction of the desperado whose cause the church officials had been championing.

During my career as a trial lawyer, their have been many situations in which my life was threatened simply because I was doing my duty in prosecuting criminals or refusing to accept bribes. There also have been a number of instances in which I have been greatly misunderstood. It is my plan to recount some of these experiences in the future.*

---

*Before completing his memoirs, Harry H. Emmons died during a massive heart attack in 1952.

Chapter III
My Formative Years

I was born in a small midwestern village of parents whose ancestry may be traced back through several American-born generations. My father, Harrison Emmons, was a Civil War veteran. He was the son of a farmer and was one of the 300,000 boys who responded to Lincoln's first call for volunteers. After Fort Sumter was fired upon, these boys voluntarily left their homes, workshops, and farms and went to the front in defense of their country.

Soon after he was honorably discharged from the infantry in 1865, Father married a young country girl, Mary Lower. They had previously met at a small railroad station during an impromptu gathering to greet President Lincoln.

71

Because of an assassination threat, the president had been advised to change his original travel plans.

After their marriage they bought an eighty-acre farm in Ringgold County, Iowa. This farm was located north of Mount Ayr, near what is now the village of Tingley. On this farm Father himself built their modest home, using simple tools. It was still standing at the time of my only visit there, in 1948.

After eight long years of hardships on this lonely farm (they were several miles from their nearest neighbors) they returned to their native Ohio. There they raised a family of nine children: William, Catherine, Albert, Delmar, Ida, Harry, Charles, James, and Mary. All of the six sons temporarily taught in one-room grade schools. Two, William S. and I (Harry H.), became lawyers and one, Charles W., a medical doctor. It may be of interest that in later years (1930s and early 1940s) William was the municipal judge of Culver City, California, and his courtroom was just across the street from the world-famous Metro-Goldwyn-Mayer motion picture studios, where many classic films have been made. During a delay in the filming of *The Wizard of Oz,* it is reported that some of the "Munchkins" became drunk and disorderly in Culver City; perhaps some may have had to appear before Judge William S. Emmons.

Father passed away in 1937, Mother having gone before, in 1934. On their joint tombstone in a little rural churchyard I had deeply engraved these words: "Lived happily together 69 years."

For three years before I was born and for approximately twenty years thereafter, Father operated a country store. It was a miniature department store, as he sold groceries, hardware, clothing, hats, boots, shoes, stationery, jewelry, fabrics, kerosene for lamps, bicycles, tobacco, cigars, and patent medicines. He also bought and shipped butter, eggs, hides, and nuts. The village post office was located near the front of the store, on one side of a large room. Father was the local postmaster under several different political administrations, and he was also the township's treasurer.

At the age of seventeen, I was appointed and sworn in as assistant postmaster, and my duties required me to be constantly in and around the post office.

Naturally our store, combined with the post office, was *the* "center of all things" in that community, and it was a very busy place from early morning until late at night. We boys and girls were all required to do our share in clerking, packing, and shipping, as well as all of the janitorial work.

Typical of all country stores of that era, our store offered a tempting place for men and boys to loaf in the afternoons and evenings—especially from fall to spring, when the menfolk had little to do. In fact, the store was used as a forum or club for these self-invited loafers, chronic and otherwise. The men congregated near the large "potbellied" cast-iron stove located in the center of the long room. There was free heat, lantern light, papers and magazines, and some chairs, nail kegs, and boxes to sit on. Occasionally Mother came into the store and was shocked and indignant to find the whole place blue with tobacco smoke from pipes and cigars. And when she noticed the unsanitary spectacle of the bespattered "spit boxes," she wasn't a bit timid in pouring out her objections in short, caustic words, pointing out the peculiar similarity between pigs and some men.

The store and post office evidently provided a very interesting place for these men to gather and spend their leisure time, sharpening and pouring out their own wit and absorbing the ideas of others. It was the focal point of the village.

Although the space around the stove was used as an improvised community forum for loafers, it often also included some well-read and intelligent men. I was usually someplace in the store where I could hear what the discussions were about. Some of these men, of course, came to make purchases, but they lingered to hear and take part in the discussions. Others came for their mail, while still others were merely loafing. All sorts of subjects, political, social, and religious, were discussed, pro and con. They criticized, argued, cussed, smoked pipes and cigars, and chewed "terbaccer." No subject was taboo, except when women were in the store and were perceived within hearing. Religion, history, politics, and current court cases concerning murders and robberies and other crimes pending in the county court provided material for earnest arguments. The subjects were always very interesting to me. Petty lawsuits then pending, and those that had already been tried before the local justices of the peace, were discussed and retried, and the witnesses, court, and jury were often mercilessly criticized. Veterans of the Civil War were usually in these groups, and their experiences (but not Father's) were told and retold so many times that they almost believed their own fantastic stories. Some listeners might have been led to think that a few of these veterans personally won the War between the States! Preachers and their sermons, teachers, and other important personages in the community were cussed and discussed. Local scandals were favorite topics, as well as such terrible crimes as certain church members going to public dances. In those days dancing was considered even more wicked than playing cards, believe it or not, as the music for the dances was made by the Devil's favorite instrument, the "fiddle." In regard to cards, Father would never sell them, although he needed the profit such sales might bring. One time when he was away on a trip I purchased a gross carton of them from a "drummer," as we had been having calls for them. But when Father returned a few days thereafter, before many of the card packages had been sold, he immediately dumped all that remained into the fire.

Around the potbellied stove, one of the most popular subjects for discussion was theology and various religious creeds. The "doubting Thomases" also made their positions clear. Free-thinkers like Thomas Paine and Robert Ingersoll were usually "given hell" in no uncertain terms, but there were also some advocates who praised them as leaders in liberal thought. All these doubting Thomases, whether atheists, agnostics, or deists, were grouped together and labeled "infidels," which in those days was a very terrifying term, and by some feared as much as smallpox. This stigma was often applied to local men whom I knew to be readers and thinkers, and who were apparently true to their own consciences. They believed at least in that part of the Bible that says: "Seek ye the truth and the truth shall make you free."

Upon hearing all these pro and con arguments, it was hard for me, as a boy, to understand and reconcile these various views and why such hard, insulting words should be applied to some who appeared to be honest and straightforward. But later on I derived some consolation and enlightenment when I read Tennyson's words: "There lives more faith in honest doubt than in half the creeds."

Some of these elderly attendants at the forum were surprisingly well read in history, science, and government. They were versed in the story of our country, the Declaration of Independence and the Constitution of the United

States, and politics in general. They were subscribers to, and read, some of the best newspapers and magazines of the day. Two or three of these farmers had fine home libraries. Others were as ignorant as could be imagined, believing in various superstitions and that the world was not round but flat.

At seventeen years of age, I formally joined our local Christian church, and I have never regretted this social and religious conformity. However, as the years passed I learned that formalities and rituals may be only superficially indicative of the inner precincts of a man's heart. I grew more liberal in my views and came to understand what Ralph Waldo Emerson meant when he said that "a man's mind is his own church."

I recall vividly one of the "doubting Thomases" who patronized our store and occasionally joined the forum, H.K.W. He was honest, well read, sincere, a good neighbor and citizen, and a kind and good father. He always wanted to do the right thing. It seemed that he was having quite a difficult time reconciling his philosophy with the general orthodox conceptions in that community. But he evidently realized the advantages to his children, then growing up, in being connected with the church. He also realized the disadvantage to his family in not being connected with the church. I remember clearly the evening H.K.W. walked down the aisle with his wife to join the church. It was a major event in the community, and, well knowing that he was an agnostic, I was carefully observing the proceedings and listening intently. H.K.W. stood up, and the minister took his hand and asked him the invariable official church question. The entire congregation was tense. Then I heard his answer: "I am trying to believe to the best of my ability."

This answer was not the answer required, but the minister, to his credit, ignored this irregularity and said, "May God bless you," and accepted him into the church. This was a happy solution to a problem that could have been so emphasized as to cause trouble in the church. In this connection I want to say that I have reason to believe that there were many members of this church who were not so honest and brave when they answered this fundamental question. H.K.W. and his family became faithful and outstanding church members and always did their share in helping to keep up the good work of the church. I have never forgotten this incident and have always admired H.K.W. for his courage in standing before that audience of two hundred or three hundred people—friends and neighbors—and risking not being accepted by the church.

People in general are growing wiser and accordingly more liberal as they realize:

> There is so much good in the worst of us,
> And so much bad in the best of us,
> That it hardly behooves any of us
> To talk about the rest of us.

Emerson said, "I like the silent church before the service begins, better than any preaching."

Of course, he was speaking figuratively, and he evidently meant that those attending church usually know what they are there for and enjoy the comfortable feeling of "being in tune with the infinite." But as soon as the minister launches into some controversial details of theology, their thoughts become confused; the comfortable, serene feeling is interrupted.

My exposure while a youth in our country store and post office, and especially in the village forum, virtually amounted to a high school education. I could say that it was my alma mater. I later read and appreciated Pencoast's writing under the title "England of the Restoration":

Coffee houses were established in great numbers and there the leading men of politics, literature and fashion met to smoke and discuss the latest sensation, over the novel luxury of coffee. Such friction made men's minds more alert, witty and alive to the newest thing. Before 1715 there were nearly two thousand of these coffee houses alone in London, representing an immense variety of classes and opinions. With the spread of intelligence and life of the club and coffee houses, the rise of periodical literature is directly connected.

Although I did not have the benefit of a formal high school education, I was able to successfully pass the county teachers' examination at seventeen years of age, and shortly thereafter I was employed for two years as a grade school teacher. I also taught another village school for one year. Then the pay was only $40.00 per month, but room and excellent board cost only $2.50 per week. My experience as a teacher also went a long way toward compensating for my lack of formal high school training. I learned while teaching, but I nevertheless felt that I had missed something, and this resulted in my having some feeling of inferiority when I started to college. Yet I soon found out that with the small amount of formal education I received in the common school as student and teacher—and the insight into human nature gained in the country store forum—I was usually capable of holding my own with the fellow students and fraternity boys on almost any subject except Latin and Greek.

Before college, in my youth, I found that, like Dante, I "was in a forest dark" and I had a strong desire to free my mind from the mud and mire of superstition and ignorance. As far back as I can remember, it seemed to me that the motto "to know is the highest ambition of mankind" was an excellent ideal. With this motto as my standard I became an omnivorous reader. At the age of fifteen, I read the Bible from cover to cover, often while sacrificing boyish pleasures such as playing ball. Then I read the orthodox *History of Christianity,* by Rev. J. F. C. Abbott; *Pilgrim's Progress,* by Bunyan, and for many years I was a constant reader of the *Christian Herald* of New York and the *Christian Standard* of Cincinnati.

I was not afraid to read anything, pro or con, as I firmly believed that in seeking the truth I would be made free. I discovered that peace of mind, one of the most desirable things in this world, can only be had through seeking and finding the truth. I read and studied, in a limited way, the wonders of astronomy, which make a man realize his own insignificance, and what a comparatively small speck of dust the Earth is. I also studied Darwin's *Origin of Species* and his *Descent of Man*, Ernest Haeckel's *Evolution of Man*, *Thomas Paine's Age of Reason*, the works of Voltaire, John Fiske's *Cosmic Philosophy,* the wonderful orations of Robert G. Ingersoll, and the writings of Benjamin Franklin, that great American philosopher, scientist, and statesman. Finally I wish to acknowledge my careful reading of Andrew D. White's two-volume *History of the Warfare of Science and Theology in Christendom,** which by itself I regard worth a liberal college education!

My extracurricular studies in science, philosophy, and especially theology, while in an orthodox church college, were oftentimes looked upon with alarm by my fellow students who knew about it. The unwritten rule seemed to be

*Editor's note: Originally published by Macmillan and Co., Ltd. in 1896; re-published by Dover Publications, Inc., New York, 1960

that the mere reading of unorthodox books amounted to a crime, and any violator of this unwritten law was regarded as dangerous. I was the only transgressor I knew of, and, to the best of my recollection, there was not another evolutionist in the entire college. But within the next twenty-five years great progress in thought along those lines was made . . . practically everyone in the college became an evolutionist, including their new president! Twenty-five years is a very short period of time for such a revolution, which sets aside the traditional thought of humanity for thousands of years.

In the years that I was teaching school and going to college, I continued my spare-time studies along the general lines of science, literature, and history. I also started directing some of my efforts to the study of law. A fellow student induced me to buy an extension course in law offered by Northwestern University of Chicago. This extension course was directed by a Dr. Cadman, author of a number of legal textbooks. I vigorously pursued this extension course and later attended Western Reserve University's Law School. In due course I successfully passed the state examination and was admitted to the bar by the state's Supreme Court on December

21, 1906. I have been practicing my chosen profession ever since. For the first seventeen years, before I relocated to a larger city, my law office was located on Main Street, downtown, in a small midwestern city. It was here where the events described in chapters 1 and 2 were centered.

In order to provide the reader additional insight into my formative years, I should next discuss some of my youthful literary efforts.

When I was about nineteen years of age, while teaching, the idea came to me that it probably would be a good thing for someone to publish a spelling book especially designed to help prospective teachers. In those days all county schoolteachers were required to take and pass a comprehensive examination. No one dared score below 70 percent. The spelling test usually consisted of about twenty-five words. I wrote to numerous county boards of examiners asking for lists of the words used in their previous examinations. My inquiry included Indiana, Illinois, Michigan, Ohio, Kentucky, Pennsylvania, West Virginia, and New York. I did not explain in my letters the purpose of my inquiry, but these boards were very generous in furnishing me with many of their different lists. By careful comparison, I found that only about one thousand words were used in all these lists. So I compiled and published my first spelling book, which I called *The Practical Speller.* The edition soon sold out, and later I published two more enlarged editions. I changed the name to *The Practical Speller and Orthography* and added several features. Announcements and advertisements were placed in various teachers' magazines; these editions also soon sold out. One teachers' college ordered 300 copies! Orders were received from practically every state in the Union and from the Hawaiian Islands, Cuba, Egypt, and the Philippines.

As my father was a rather poor man and as he had a large family to support, I received very little financial help from him. And I did not expect any after starting to college. I had to earn my own livelihood and pay my own tuition and expenses. This was very difficult at times, and so I tried many different ways to earn money. My methods included some freelance writing.

One beautiful Sunday morning I attended a nearby Christian church. The speaker on that occasion was a very fine-looking elderly gentleman, and he preached an interesting sermon. I noticed that he needed no glasses for reading, nor did he use a cane. I thought what a fine physical example he represented. Upon inquiry I learned that he was Rev. Harrison Jones and that he was over ninety years of age at that time. I also learned that he was a nationally known figure, having officiated at the funeral of President Garfield. The thought struck me that this man's life would make an interesting story. So the following day I found and interviewed him. He told me about the days when, as a young circuit-rider minister, he rode horseback from one parish to another, that he never used liquor or tobacco in any form, and that he had always been temperate in his habits and even-tempered in his disposition. In short, he attributed his good health and long life to those habits. He also gave me a fine large photograph of himself. I wrote up this story and sent it and the photograph to *Physical Culture* magazine, which was then in its infancy. The story was accepted and was published with a full-page photograph of Reverend Jones. To my great satisfaction I received a nice letter and the personal check from Bernarr MacFadden, the famous editor and publisher.*

The editor of our college's monthly magazine

*Editor's footnote: Bernarr MacFadden (1868-1955) Ref. *Who Was Who in America*, v. III at various times asked me to write articles for their readers. Two essays I contributed were titled "Independence in Politics" and "The Origin of Language and the Influence of Authors." In the latter I included the well-known quotation: "All that mankind has done, thought, gained or been is lying as in magic preservation in the pages of books. They are the chosen possession of men."

Then, in the spring of 1900, when I was not yet twenty-two years of age, I was studying one warm afternoon out under a large tree on our college campus. I remember that it was a very beautiful day, and after finishing my studies I sat there reflecting on the beauties and marvels of nature. This inspired me to write, without benefit of reference books or notes, an article on the subject "Reflections on Nature," which I submitted to the *Word and Works* magazine of Saint Louis. This was a monthly magazine that had been published for more than twenty-five years, which was then edited by Rev. Earl R. Hicks. The general purpose of the magazine was to reconcile modern science, especially astronomy, with religion. When this article was published in the June issue of 1900, I received numerous complimentary letters from all over the United States. But above all of these letters, I remember that of a minister twice my age who hunted me up and highly complimented my article, saying that he had been reading this magazine for many years and that my article was the best he had ever read in it. This was very encouraging to me, and I am sure it helped reduce my feelings of inferiority. I make no special claim for this article now, but I will include it here, be it good or bad:

Reflections on Nature

Only the truly great realize fully the littleness of all human achievements. When we compare man and his works to nature, the former sinks into nothingness; when we think of the magnitude of the universe and of the wonders of the world, as science reveals them to us, we, as it were, get lost in our own imaginations. Oh, how great is creation! Think about it, read about it, or, if you please, make its study a specialty and still it is beyond your comprehension or even your apprehension. Its size can only be described by the words, "it is without limit." We look at our Earth and think it is gorgeous, but when we consider that it would take one million, three hundred thousand Earths to make a Sun our globe seems but a pygmy. Yet this is only one of the many millions of suns that are larger than our terrestrial sphere, and this is only one illustration of the comparative littleness of man's habitation. On this same line, let us reflect on other marvels. Imagine the Moon revolving around the Earth; the Earth around the Sun; the Sun around another center; and this center obeying the same law around still another greater body, and so on throughout endless space. Some of these bodies, which are far beyond the reach of the most powerful telescopes, are so remote from us that it would take light traveling at the rate of one hundred eighty-six thousand miles per second hundreds of millions of years to reach us. It takes over eight years for light to come from Sirius, the Dog Star, which is estimated to be about fifty trillions of miles from us. The distance to the nearest fixed star is such that it takes over four years for its light to reach Earth. The most distant stars visible to the naked eye are estimated to be about seven hundred forty trillions of miles away, and thus rays of light we see took about one hundred twenty-five years to reach us.

Old Nature everywhere exhibits many prodigies, and we need not look to other worlds to see the manifestation of her phenomena when we are surrounded on all sides by her wonders. For example, let us look at some very simple illustrations. In twenty-four hours, under favorable circumstances fourteen hundred million microbes will spring from a single germ. Think how many that is—about as many as there are people in the whole world. In an average square yard of carpet there is estimated to be between ten and thirty-five million microbes. On an ordinary dog, which is kept comparatively clean, too, there are over a hundred million of these infinitesimal beings. At every breath we take, twenty million discs die in our blood, and as many spring into life. The human heart throbs at the rate of one hundred thousand beats per day, forty million a year, and often three billion without a single stop. The machinery of the body is the most wonderful of all machines. If the heart should expend its whole force in lifting itself vertically it would rise two thousand feet an hour. The greatest feat of a locomotive was to lift itself through less than one-eighth of that distance in the same time.

Such illustrations show us the marked contrast between Nature and man; and when we contemplate these facts which are common to us all, and realize with what harmony, regularity, and precision Nature performs her duties, we are almost bewildered with our own insignificance. With such musings on the perfection of Nature, the mind of man can account for her precision and harmony only by concluding that there is a power presiding over the Universe and that Power is God.

The day I was admitted to the bar by the state Supreme Court, an incident occurred that inspired me to write a short note for the *National Tribune,* a newspaper published in Washington, D.C., in the interests of the federal veterans of the Civil War and their families. Practically every member of the Grand Army of the Republic was a subscriber and, therefore, this paper had a large circulation. I wrote this note on what was, to me, a memorable day in 1906:

A Tribute to Soldiers

A few days ago I was admitted to the bar of my state. I took my oath before that most august body, the Supreme Court, the most highly dignified institution in this great Commonwealth. I walked out of the court room with my diploma, feeling proud of my achievement, and, as it were, patting myself on the back, going directly into the relic room of the Capitol. I glanced around a few minutes until my eyes fell on something very interesting, indeed. It was two old worn-out tat-

tered regimental flags which my father followed
for over three long years through the great Civil
War. I stood there fully fifteen minutes and gazed
and thought. My mind went back to the darkest
days of the Nation's history. I saw my father, a
young man, following those old tattered rags up
Lookout Mountain, bloody Missionary Ridge, at
Chickamauga, and at Chattanooga. I saw him on
the field of battle fighting for honor, for home, for
his country and for the freedom of 4,000,000
people, in the twenty-some battles in which he
served. I saw his nearest comrades shot down
and his dearest companions wasted by disease
and removed by death. I saw him before and
during battles, thinking of home, of friends, of
his sweetheart—my mother now—and wonder-
ing with agonizing torture if he would ever see
their faces again. I saw him return home at the
end of the terrible conflict, but only the shadow
of the robust young man he was four years before, and with his future dark and uncertain.
And then, with almost tears in my eyes, when I
thought again of the noble work of soldiers, of
their stout souls and strong hearts, of the patri-
otic courage it took in such ordeals of hell, of the
freeing of the four million slaves and thereby
preventing the enslavement of hundreds of millions of unborn human beings, I said that my
accomplishments are nothing: that a soldier in

such a holy war is greater than any lawyer who ever lived, than any poet who ever wrote, than any king who ever breathed.

To my surprise, I received numerous complimentary letters from all over the United States. Along with the letters, I received several invitations from official committees to deliver their May 30, 1907, Memorial Day address. I accepted one of these invitations, and since this was to be my first public speech after becoming a lawyer, I prepared meticulously. The speech went well and I was given a nice reception. I remember this as one of the most pleasant occasions of my young life, while I began my practice as a Main Street lawyer in the early 1900s.

Postscript by Author's Son
(1996)

Attorney Harry H. Emmons (1878–1952) was a highly respected member of his county and state bar associations and of the Unitarian Fellowship. During his professional career he published several books. Among them are the first book of classified phrases in the United States, *Smart Words and Phrases* (1908); a highly acclaimed anthology, *Master Thoughts* (1926); and, in 1930, both *Light of Emerson* and *Philosograms of Emerson*. In these latter two volumes my father showed his deep admiration for Ralph Waldo Emerson, describing him as "America's greatest literary genius." At the request of the Emerson Club of Cleveland, Ohio, my father addressed their 1931 banquet, choosing as his topic, "Emerson, the American Confucius." Following are a few of the many "Philosograms" that my father like to quote:

> Hitch your wagon to a star.
> Make yourself necessary to somebody.
> He alone is rich who owns the day.
> 'Tis the good reader that makes the good book.
> Life is a succession of lessons which must be
>   lived to be understood.
> All that I have seen teaches me to trust the
>   Creator for all I have not seen.

In his published personal "Creed of Life" (1931), Harry H. Emmons included among his cardinal points this egalitarian wish: "To grant to others all joys, rights and privileges I desire for myself." My father was a cheerful friend of all who sought truth, justice, and a better world.

—Richard Harrison Emmons

Harry H. Emmons (1878–1952)